BORIS BY THE SEA

BORIS BY THE SEA
by Matvei Yankelevich

Octopus Books
Denver, Colorado/Portland, Oregon
2009

OCTOPUS
BOOKS

The author would like to acknowledge the editors of the periodicals in which some Borises originally appeared: Dana Ward of *Cypress Magazine*; Libby Hodges, et al., at *St. Petersburg Review*; and Zachary Schomburg of *Octopus Magazine*. Andrey Gritsman included some pieces in the anthology *Stranger at Home* (Ars-Interpres, 2008); and Aaron Petrovich and Alex Rose gave Boris a room in the *Hotel St. George*. About one quarter of the Borises originally appeared in the artist's book, *Borises by the Sea* (2000), designed and printed by Ellie Ga in a limited edition of fifty copies at Women's Studio Workshop, Rosendale, New York. Parts of *Boris by the Sea* served as the basis for a theater piece of the same title, conceived and directed by Daniel Kleinfeld and staged twice in New York City in 1999 (at Henry Street Settlement, as part of the Fringe Festival, and at HERE Arts Center) with his intrepid players Dima Dubson, Rika Daniel, Peter Brown, Oleg Dubson, David Salper, Michelle Kovacs, and Julie Halpern, sound designer Todd Polenberg, costumer Elizabeth Goodman, and dramaturg Yelena Gluzman.

Boris by the Sea

First edition, 2009; Second printing, 2010
ISBN: 978-0-9801938-2-4
Printed & bound in the USA

Cover design by Denny Schmickle
www.dennyschmickle.com

Octopus Books
Denver, Colorado & Portland, Oregon
www.octopusbooks.net

Titles set in Avenir. Text set in Sabon.

TO ELLIE AND YOZHKA

I

+

Boris was thirsty so he watered his plants. When the plants died from being over-watered Boris was still thirsty. Boris had no more plants to water so he watered the sand that was left. The water sat in the sand and went nowhere.

Boris was still thirsty.

Boris went outside and watered the sea while no one was looking. The sea waved and nodded and waved again. But Boris was even thirstier. And the sea was no different for it.

Boris had no water left. He rolled in the sand and became dirty.

+

Boris lay flat on the ground and began to watch things happen. It started slow. But things were definitely afoot. Boris got a crazy idea in his head to build something and he began with himself. He said to his right foot, Build yourself. And it did. The left foot followed suit. It got boring.

He thought he might build something else but what.

A chair.

He started by thinking about what it should look like, what is a chair, what makes it a chair. When he opened his eyes he saw it there before him. And when he closed his eyes again he fell asleep and dreamed of things he could never build in his room, things he would never see before him once he opened his eyes.

+

Boris lived in his room and thought about why people need each other. People need each other, thought Boris, to check each other for ticks. People need each other for solving the problem of what is inside.

Boris looked himself over and realized there were many parts of him that he could not see. And only a small part of these parts was on the surface. The urge to rip out one's own heart arises from this, he thought.

Boris dreamt of men who disattached their thoughts from the government of their own organisms. These men could, if they happened to notice their own body, consider it to be somebody else's body and open it up to see what was inside. The surface is never enough for such men.

But people need each other to open each other up and see what is inside. And to scratch their backs.

Boris reached around and touched his shoulder blade. He wondered what it looked like. He got a good hold on it. He pulled hard. And he pulled harder. But he could not bring it around to the front.

EQUATION OF A KITTEN

Boris did nothing because it was wicked.

He hardly thought — that might get him in trouble with Woman.

The fine laundry on display shone brightly in the sun. She washed it and she dried it. She was water and warmth. Was that what Woman was.

That was not what Woman was to Boris. To Boris she was neither rain nor shine. She was fake as wooden sheep, false as snowflakes, fraudulent as kitten sneezes.

Woman was white. All white. Pearly smooth, to wit.

+

Whenever Boris was alone in his room he wasn't. He wasn't alone being alone in the room. He was with. He was with hat. He was with eyes and ears. He was with walls. He was with time. He was with him. He had been with her and that made her absence.

Whenever he was alone that way time went by. It went by like a river just keeps going by. It doesn't stop even when you catch it. Even when you notice the moment it goes by. Even if you ask politely. It won't give you the time of day. It won't give you any time at all. No time to yourself.

Whenever time went by Boris, Boris felt it going by, much the way a rock feels the river going by, changing him a little at a time, but constantly always changing him as it goes by. And not for a moment can he stop it from changing him, not for a minute can he stop it from going by. He cannot stop changing as the river goes by. So Boris was like a rock in the river, ever-changing. He could not stop time from going by, he could not invite it to stay a while, to rest. It accepted no invitation. It must flow on. It is urgent.

+

Boris lay in bed sweating. The world was reflected inside him, somewhere inside his skull. And it hurt. It hurt something awful. Boris lay in bed and thought: is it my skull that is hurting, or is it the world around me that has fallen ill. The chair, the soup, the table, and the ceiling, and the lid from something or other, all of it hurts. Even the wallpaper groans and creaks from the pain. If you don't look at the world then your headache will go away, thought Boris. And everything vanished in the room. All the things died and the dead do not complain. They are no longer in pain.

+

So Boris stopped what he was doing and began to live alone. He kicked everyone out. And he said, This is worse for me, but better for everyone. And he was scorned.

Boris was not always this way. Before he was like everybody else, and he could say:

— What should I do.

and

— Should I do.

and also

— I do.

These things got him into trouble with Woman.

But not only that. Other things too.

THE METAPHYSICS OF A BORIS BY THE SEA

Boris looked at his hand and could not identify whose hand it was.

+

Boris felt that he could not grasp reality.

It glimmered outside the window in questions' broken branches.

And he began to bite his fingers. He started with his nails, first his pinkie. He had bitten through all his nails. Only their traces were left. And he proceeded to rid himself of the traces. He bit off the tip of his pinkie and thought: But it will stick in my stomach! What sort of thing is this. In this manner I will never rid myself of the traces of chewed-off finger nails.

And he spit out the tip of his pinkie into a glass.

On the windowsill by the table by the chair where he sat by the door which was next to the window where, in the dust, stood the glass into which Boris had spit out the tip of the finger which he had bitten off from himself.

Slowly a dark thought came over Boris: In such a manner Boris could be rid of himself. And then for the first time in his life Boris said aloud: There is a limit to everything everywhere.

+

Boris was at the bar, but nobody knew it. It was a seaside sort of affair. Was he waiting for a sign. The neon buzzed and lit his face pale.

There was a there that was there, a real there there, and some folks were there, and you could basically have a drink there, if you were already there. He was there.

A long sentence followed.

It took a while to get going. But once he got going, he was pretty much gone.

He had waited enough. He would wait no more. Then he waited some more.

Does Boris stumble out of the bar — if so, for what purpose. To grow dark. To go back. To be sought for.

+

Boris wanted to know about kissing. He wanted to know why and how it all got startead.

— Was it dental hygiene.

— Was it pleasure.

— How did the first people stumble upon the first kiss.

Boris decided to run some tests on the kiss. There was no one around. Woman had disappeared. She was coming back. He looked at his watch. Eternity.

Boris began to kiss himself. His lower lip stretched out toward his upper lip. It, in turn, dove downward. They met in a tight embrace and caressed each other. Mushed thick mass against thin skin, pushing the blood out, sucking it back in. He felt a sharp pain between his front teeth. He pulled his lips back. He got bored of it. It was getting late. He wound the clocks. He had not done this for a long time. Woman was late in arriving. When she did he was already gone, the day done. She looked under the bed. She closed her eyes and saw Boris. His mouth was a cave gaping wide. And she looked down into his throat. She went in and closed the door behind her. She was safe here from the rain and bad jobs and hardness. She cuddled in the wet blanket and put her head on an ivory pillow.

She was inside him now. Boris took a deep breath. He was all set. Nothing more. He listened to the footsteps of the rising tide rolling pebbles in-between its toes. Falling, standing still. They came no closer. They went no farther than their limits.

He closed his eyes and died quietly a man in a room by the sea.

IN THE LANGUAGE OF THE THEATER (AN EXPERIMENT)

PART I

> BORIS (*form of woman*):
>
>> I walk on stage. I become a duckling.
>>
>> I wrap myself in a toga. I am a child speaking.

Enter Boris (form of woman). Boris makes a chair out of her knee for Boris to sit on.

> BORIS (*form of woman*):
>
>> I sit alone on stage. It's empty. Darkness. Utter.
>>
>> Where are those butterflies that in my stomach flew and fluttered
>>
>> with their wings making me nauseous,
>>
>> and the nervous state in the audience...

Boris ceases talking about himself — he is suddenly overcome by a feeling, as if a weight had been lifted off him, as when death comes in your sleep or as though he had gone away to the sea.

At this time all the other Borises in the form of women gather around the first ones, coming slowly out of the darkness. They move smoothly, like ocean waves, like the tide and the sand and the pebbles, smooth.

PART II

> BORIS: We must not forget how to speak.

+

Now Boris had his own. His own jacket, his own boot, his own forte-piano, his own collar, his own time, his own money, even his own room in his own apartment bungalow.

Boris had his own life. This life stood around Boris like an eyeless room, not a door nor a window. There was no way in or out. Not for Boris, nor for anyone else. This pleased him because he could do nothing, and nothing could do anything to him. He paid no heed whether sleet snow wind rain or shine, he was always in his own element.

Now Boris was on his own.

+

The clouds passed over thick with oil. Boris wasn't sure he should go outside. It became dark. The thunder struck his eardrums.

Boris thought that he had died, but actually he was just someone else.

Another Boris. In another room. By another sea. How many of us are there, thought Boris. And the one I once was, where is he now. Also replaced by another Boris.

Boris tried to remember the words to something, but his mind was tired. He opened the door once more and looked up. The sky's gray belly hung big and low. Along the shoreline Boris could see the smeared lines of forest and beach where the rain had already started falling.

The sun shone through crevices between the clouds, peeking at Boris. He leaned out of the doorway and looked down the row of beachfront homes. In the doorway of the neighboring bungalow he saw the balding pate of a fellow vacationer. He too was leaning out to see what was doing further down where another such man peered cautiously out the doorway to see what was with the weather.

Boris felt a pain, and an itch, and then a general discomfort, and then: thirst. He waited for the rain to come closer. He sat and waited. None came.

The clouds were thick with water, greedy clouds. Give it to me, he wanted to say but he couldn't remember the words. He wanted to be polite about it.

The dry season appeared rapping on his window with a fist full of sand.

Some day, he thought, I will die of this thirst and then what.

II

THE SECOND PREFACE

I hope that Boris will help me in this respect.
Perhaps the theater holds for us an important truth:
that without a role a person is as good as dead.

People want someone to lie beside them.
When there's someone else under the blanket,
in the dark, then you know who you are
in relation to that someone who lies beside you.

Who am I alone. Missing my role.
I'm afraid I might leave this world behind.
I hope that Boris will help me in this respect.

BY THE SEA, THE TWAIN MEET (A PLAY)

Dramatis Personae:

Author (a Chekhovian gentleman)
Tripod (three distracted women)
Boris (a mephistophelian cad)
SUBTOTAL: 2 men and 3 wom.
TOTAL: 5 pers.

AUTHOR: A foreign writer once met his own invention in a park — no, his double! The one I wanted to become, the one I desired to be! It was our first meeting in the park. He was standing by a photographic camera. He snapped a picture of me. Suddenly.

BORIS: Cheese!

AUTHOR: What are you doing here?

BORIS: I am trying to catch the moment.

AUTHOR: You're doing what?

BORIS: I'm taking pictures.

AUTHOR (*looks out at the audience from behind the tripod made of three women*): Well, I'll be. You sonofabitch. (*Aside:*) He spoke as I could not. He thought in ways I could not myself think.

BORIS: I was just thinking, wouldn't it be nice if I stopped time?

AUTHOR: Yes?

BORIS: Time goes along at a certain speed. (*He looks at his watch.*) It does a minute in 60 seconds. Can't you count it? One, two, three... 5... 19... If we were to catch time by its tail and go along at the same speed as time, then —

AUTHOR: — at this point I interrupted him — I'm afraid there's an imperfection here...

BORIS: I agree — I must take a picture. Watch the birdie! (*Boris snaps a picture and a flashbulb explodes.*) It is precisely this imperfection in time which gives us this possibly impossible opportunity. In general, I am perfecting imperfection.

AUTHOR: What?

BORIS: You're impossible! You'd think he'd think for himself sometime. But no, I've got to do it.

AUTHOR: Yes. You want to correct time. To perfect it means to stop it. Time in motion is flimsy like the wind, unstable like an acrobat on a wire.

BORIS: You got me all wrong. Imperfections must be perfected, but not corrected. Ridding himself of imperfections, a man dies, or rather Life does. Look at a woman of perfection — she will not love you, nor you her. The imperfect must be guarded. Perfection destroys us and our thoughts. Take imperfect thoughts to their limits, to complete imperfection, exhaust imperfection... About time — you made that up yourself.

Boris distances himself.

AUTHOR (*to Boris*): That's impossible. (*Aside:*) And how easy it really is for the impossible to happen.

Author is carried away on many hands.

The next scene is to be played upside-down.

+

Boris, back when he could think, once thought the following thought: Nothing should ever be finished, nothing and never. Right. And no need to. Anyway, all that exists in the world will always stay on, you can't get rid of the world. More likely, it, the world, is infinite seeing as it has no end. All that lives and dies in the world stays in it. You can't get rid of the dead. It lies heavily on the earth.

THE CROSSING

Boris had to have a talk to Ivan, serious. He sat down again and Ivan stood up again as if they had been sitting and standing, respectively. Indeed they had, as usual. On Boris's lap there was still a page of the novel which he was writing which had no words.

Ivan interpreted this and said: When you will write the novel will the novel be a reflection of the real world or will it be a separate world which you have created.

Boris decided he would play along. He played along and along and a long time after he realized he had a grasp on things especially with respect to nothing, things with no meaning to them, and he had already developed the following philosophy: that of the world of maximum possibilities.

Being doubtful gave him the upper hand: he could answer twice to every question. And he did.

Boris began to imagine a world where things were real because we believed in them, and then he told Ivan that this world where reality and solid forms were such because we thought them so, that this was our real world. This made Ivan cross. In effect Boris was saying that the world that he was writing was an independent world but was just as real as this real world which was just as make-believe as the world he was writing. And both were reflections of each other and could not exist in total isolation. That's really all he was saying.

But that wasn't all. Boris remembered that he wasn't writing a novel with words: he was writing a novel without words. But he didn't say anything about it to Ivan. He kept it to himself.

+

When Boris still thought he thought that he could not think when someone was looking. Especially Woman. Woman is watching him and he cannot think. So he stopped thinking, because someone, usually Woman, was watching him.

Then she left. Boredom set in. And then he thought and understood that to think and to create something resembles defecating and peeing. Both are preferably done alone.

Woman had gone and Boris thought about all this for some time. And he peed in the privacy of his own toilet.

IN THE AUTHOR'S KITCHEN

How egocentric is the author. He thinks that he can save his characters.

How horrible it would be if one of them said: You saved me, I didn't hang myself because of you.

How horrible! Why didn't you hang yourself? And why because of me? How unpleasant.

There was a song in my childhood — oh how egocentric I am! Is it not egocentric to speak of my childhood as one might speak of another's childhood? — The song went: He writes it how he hears it.

The author is so egocentric: he doesn't care anymore which language he writes in!

How egocentric is the author! He writes for the theater and imagines that his words will be manifested and flung wildly from the stage with masterful freedom by trained actors with colorful lives who do not stutter, who speak without obstruction.

This is how egocentric he is: he permits us to dispose of him, and for this alone he is in love with himself.

How egocentric is the author — not joining the ranks of a theatrical movement!

This is how egocentric the author is! And the characters, what can they do, how can they live after the show, after the book is closed shut? How, how?

+

Boris wondered if he had been made wrong.

He checked to see if any parts were missing. Seems to be all here. Everything seems to be in its place.

But he certainly felt wrong. There was no way to tell. Boris wondered for a little while longer. He was distracted by the air moving around him. It smelled of salt and fish.

+

I wanted to write about guts and intestines and other human innards, but then I found out that someone had already written about that. Then I got an idea to write about mystical letters, about the aleph, about the letter I, about a man made of clay, and about a man hanging upside-down.

And then I remembered: that had also been written about. And then I decided to write about something so very far away from all of this. But either it didn't work out or I had a strange feeling that that had also already been written about, and even that there was quite a lot written on that subject. Seized by a fleeting moment, I began writing about what I had planned to write about but which had already been written about.

But, it seems, others have already written about that, too. Only, I haven't written about that yet... about that which I myself had not written about for this or that reason.

But these lists became nothing more than mere enumerations of that which was not mine — the already written, already thought of, the has-been-done of others. Soon I will come to the understanding that language, when you are writing it, tends to choose its own subject — its own about what. What is being written about, what the words refer to. I will crave for wider strokes. The thirst for writing will be quenched, albeit by bloodshed. And then it begins: I write about everything at once. And language will forget about its definitions and cease clarifying for the reader what exactly the author wrote about and thought about. What he will write, and what he will think.

And maybe the author will not think, perhaps he won't think at all, and

+

Ok, Boris, Ivan said, you are a dead end.

But Boris couldn't see the connection, himself and the last leg.

Boris said, And yet, I am still Boris. Is that what you mean. I'm just getting started. Then I will keep going. I'll end up someday. And that'll be that. That'll be it.

+

Boris went to the sea. The water was dirty.

He put his hands in the white sand and brushed them clean.

He put his hands in the water now. They disappeared into the green.

He rubbed them together, pushing the water this way and that.

He thought he might try a washboard.

A man's voice called for him from the bungalow apartment. Who was calling him. Was he calling himself. Where. Home.

But he was busy. He was washing the water.

The voice was like a saw. It jiggled. It cut.

Perhaps it was the wind, I thought, as I kicked the pebbles and the sand. Perhaps there is a draft, thought I, and lifted up my hand.

But there was no draft — because there was no door. Unless the author wandering the beach took Boris for the door.

But he was washing the water. Nothing came of it.

The water frothed between his hands and a white foam rose to the surface.

The white foam was white. But it was not clean.

Boris gave up washing the water. One should never give up. So he tried again.

+

If people were to see Boris out on the street they might bump up next
to him or come up close against his pockets. And they would see the tiny
cockroaches crawling over his ears and cuff links.

+

Boris had an itch:

He scratched at the itch, and around the itch, and through the itch, and into the itch. He scratched until it went away. He scratched at the itch all day.

The next day it was still there. Itchier than ever. Boris determined that the itch was part of him, just like the thought of the itch was part of him. He scratched away at the thought of the itch, took away the better part of the day and another day was scratched away in this way.

In vain! cried the walls and the moldings.
In vain! cried the doors to the doormats.
In vain! cried the ceilings and fixtures.
In vain! cried the rain.
In vain! cried Ivan, wherever Ivan went.

And so the story goes out with Ivan's container and into a taxonomy of reverberations. Wave upon wave hit the itchy shore. Scratching at the sand.

So everything scratches, In vain, in vain. And the weather scratches the weather vein.

Once you start scratching, you just can't stop. The author reflected upon this thought.

+

Boris wasn't sure where he was going. For a moment he thought that he was in the middle of a sentence. The next minute he found himself walking down an empty street. Just then he was not trampled (barely) by a harnessed mare pulling along a crumbling carriage. Suddenly Boris became very old. And wise too.

But then, as it happens some of the time with old and wise men, Boris fell over dead. At this point the story comes to a point, and that point is too narrow for the story to pass through.

+

One of his guests brought Boris a plant. Boris decided that he would watch it grow. He sat in front of it for a long time but nothing seemed to happen. He sat for even longer, and still nothing happened. The guest came to visit Boris again. Boris came to the door, but said that he was busy.

With what, said the guest.

With the plant, said Boris.

Oh, said the guest, and left.

Boris came back to the plant. Miraculously, it had grown a new sprout, and that sprout had grown the beginnings of a bud. Boris knew that something had happened. His faith was restored. He sat down to watch the plant again. Again nothing happened. Boris got older and the plant got older, too. But neither grew. Instead, Boris fell asleep. He was awakened by the plant. The bud had blossomed and the flower now stroked Boris's brow in a tickling way. But Boris wasn't at all tickled, he was angry at himself. Then he got angry at the plant, too.

He showed the plant the door and closed it behind the plant.

The guest came over again and knocked on the door.

Boris came to the door.

Are you busy, said the guest's voice.

Oh, it's you, said Boris. Come in, he said, and opened the door.

There stood the guest. He was holding the plant.

You forgot this outside, said the guest, extending the plant to Boris.

I hadn't forgot it, said Boris.

FOREWORD

Who am I.

Recently this question did not worry me in the least.

It didn't even come up.

I thought that it wasn't even worth thinking about.

But when I lie awake at night under the blanket it is so dark

that I can't see myself. I begin to touch myself —

I haven't disappeared. Yes, that's for sure. I haven't disappeared.

But who is that.

+

Boris found out from the window long before us what fate is.

Fate is nothing.

And the thingness around us circles like crows as magpies.

It was never as beautiful at the cemetery as when you were dying.

Boris had no parents — he appeared.

Or maybe he just doesn't remember them.

He simply had no faith in the past.

And he didn't go there.

+

Boris wore his clothes out. The world is my doorstop, he said. Boris worried about the draft. The one that brought all the wrong diseases. Boris feared the draft. Which side would it come from. Would it touch his back or his front, his left or his right. The draft could come from anywhere. He kicked away the doorstop and let the door shut closed. There must have been a draft, he concluded, seeing the way the door closed shut, but now there is none.

+

There is nothing particular about Boris.

He's particular to nothing.

THE CROSSING CONTINUING

That's when Boris sat down in his chair. Once upon a time Boris had written a poem without syllables. Now he took that poem and pasted it into the epigraph space on the page on his lap. Now he had an epigraph. All that was left was the novel. Having sat down with the page on his lap Boris had already commenced writing a novel. He decided that the novel would be without words.

The novel appeared slowly on the page on his lap. Boris had always been confident. Now he was still confident. The draft no longer worried him. The poem with no syllables was inspiring. He could not get anywhere with it. The novel... Ivan walked in and interrupted the novel with no words with a word. Hello, he said. Ivan rolled the world back in with him. He propped it up against the door. A draft blew chills down Boris's throat, thrilling quivers.

They quarreled. Not this time, but before. Now Ivan long since longing for revenge loved the world and that was revenge enough. He had a feather in his cap and the cap was so tightly sewn to his hair that he was not ever afraid of the wind. The wind might have knocked it off before, but not now. Ivan had the upper hand. He held it over Boris. This was a greeting, degrading.

Then Boris knocked something over. It all to pieces fell and was no more. No more would there be anything over the floor to be knocked. No more was there anything in Boris's room at all. Except for Boris. And a bit more — Ivan.

+

Boris was in a diner. Only it was the wrong diner.

The right diner was aluminum blue, it was heavy inside, it had revolving tables and formica chairs, it had a soft cushion floor and potted flowers in the porthole windows. But this diner where Boris happened to be was not like that at all. They don't make diners by the sea, at least not the right kind of diner.

Boris saw the light. There were many of them, little lights everywhere making one big blinking bright mess of white.

When it was over he had a headache. And yet it was never over. It followed him, it persisted, it straggled, it blurred left and right. Boris followed, making circles.

+

Boris imagined a world in which everything was real.

Once this world was very beautiful.

The radio played and no one listened. Why was it playing, and for whom.

Somehow it's unclear where it came from and who turned it on.

It got dark.

It used to be light.

— When it was light.

— When.

NOTE:

If one is to write a children's book, one should avoid picturing a human in the illustrated world of the book. The illustrations should be abstract color washes or designs and portray the objects that occupy the world without ever showing the human himself. Not even his hands or any human thing should be shown. The rest of the characters perhaps even should not be shown, perhaps only attributes of their personas. Things should occupy this world. Things are materialized thoughts. This is the real-ation of things: chairs, matchbooks, sand, water, windows, wind, drafts, doors, keyholes (photographic cameras), plants, watering cans, pens, paths, and holes.

Thank you!

The Author.

+

Boris sat on the floor thinking about the past. I have written a lot of things now, thought Boris, and there is still one thing I have not figured out. Boris thought about what that thing could be. Then he understood what he could not understand. I have not figured out, he said to himself, what words have to do with it.

+

Is there anything real about Boris?

Better to wonder, is there anything abstract about Boris?

Coming back to Boris, does Boris ever come back?

Does he stay away, instead?

Ivan, standing erect in the doorway.

Boris, stooping to the window.

The wind drives the sand.

How old are we, really?

How close are we, really?

How least? How spun? How in jest?

||||

✝

Boris took the chair apart. He made the parts into a pile. He lit a match. As the parts were wooden, they began to burn. Boris threw the matches in, too. They were also wooden and also began to burn.

He watched and watched as the parts burned and burned. He was satisfied just to watch. The chair seemed also strangely satisfied, as though it had finally fulfilled its true purpose. And Boris had helped it to do so. And when it was finished there was a charred black hole in the wooden floor where once a chair had stood. And Boris climbed into the hole.

THE AUTHOR

There has never
been a time in
which I have been
convinced from
within myself
that I am alive.

Truly, when I believed
in it, everything disappeared.

What do people talk about,
asked Boris.

It is true —
the only categories left are
nice and not nice —
and these persuade our natures
to bend and break
and to be good.

There was also: how it used to be
which was, for the most part,
nice.

If it happened not to be (nice)
then it was certainly much better
now.

+

The tram stopped. The driver turned the motor off.
And opened the door. He peered out — Any passengers.
Boris shouted that. A mute woman got off the tram
having first explained with her hands that she felt the hopelessness
of the street traffic. The tram in the intersection goes nowhere.
A cheapskate plot. Boris sat intermittently tearing
the buds' newly protruding pale-green cabbage off the trees
with his glances — not even leaving the tram.
The tram stood still. And time stood still.
Someone was dangling their feet. Perhaps it was time itself.
— Time is always restless, thought Boris.

+

Author:

I can see it now.

Boris is angry. He is angry that love is not like in the songs. That she can be next to him and nothing can be happening. That he does not dream of her. That love is not crazy.

He wanted something sweet.

Then he wanted something salty.

Then he might want something sweet again.

He said something.

She understood something else.

+

In fact there was nothing to keep him from opening it. Nothing but the imagined threat of what he imagined might step out once he did it. Sometimes the imagined affects our actions more than the real. This was the case. Were he to find it empty the doors would have been unnecessary and therefore frightening in their enormous uselessness.

+

Boris is missing.

      I looked for him in the grass

      in the wardrobe

      in myself

Where did he go.

+

The Author woke up one morning and wrote down all the things he had to do. Then he looked at his finger. The same finger he had had all his life at the end of his hand. All his life he had pointed at things with this finger, asking what they were. But he had never asked about his finger. A finger like any other, it should not have given him any pause. To think, even this day. But there it was, a finger at the end of his hand, extended and breaking at the edge into the end of him. He examined it closely and saw a singular finger. He tried pointing at this and that, but all he could see was his finger. Everything was his finger. Everything he touched now was a finger. A long time passed for everyone. He went through the list, moving his finger down the page. So much to do, so much to do.

+

Boris had an idea. Then he sat down and wept. It is hard to say what it was that Boris had been thinking about before he stopped thinking about it. He closed the window.

IN MEMORY OF

BORIS YANKELEVICH (1950–2002)

AND

EFREM YANKELEVICH (1950–2009)